# THE HOLY GHOST PEOPLE

T0275502

THE HOLY GHOST PEOPLE
© 2014 Joshua Young

Published by Plays Inverse Press
Pittsburgh, PA
www.playsinverse.com

ISBN 13: 978-0-9914183-0-5

First Printing: February 2014
Cover art and design by Ryan Spooner
Book design by Tyler Crumrine
Printed in the U.S.A.

PLAYS
INVERSE

# THE HOLY GHOST PEOPLE
## JOSHUA YOUNG

PLAYS INVERSE PRESS
PITTSBURGH, PA
2014

*for Elliot*

HOLY GHOST PEOPLE – a group of men & women who claim to have traveled through space & time to share the true word of god with the people of earth. they walk around in white flowing cloth. the holy ghost people distrust what the people of earth claim to be god & they mistrust what the people of earth claim to be science. they claim to know, & to have been sent by, the real god.

SPEAKERS – men & women who live on earth. they do not necessarily believe in the god the holy ghost people accuse them of believing in.

POLICEMEN – kind of annoyed with the holy ghost people.

A BARFLY – drinks.

we'll come in at the half-act & the holy ghost
people will be here already, their clothes whip-
ping in the windchill.

The Half-Act.

## SCENE I

**CURTAIN RISES,** *revealing* DARKNESS.

*Beyond the* DARKNESS *is a small city neighborhood of brick & small lawns. There is an empty highway, an abandoned car. There is an empty beach. There is an empty playground. There is a nearly deserted mall parking lot. There is a small brick church with a garden surrounding it. There is a farmers' market. There is an apartment building. There is an empty bar.*

*The center is* DARK. *The surroundings are* DARK. SPOTLIGHTS *cut holes in the* DARKNESS *& fade to black at the end of each scene.*

SPOTLIGHT – *The apartment building.*

*There is a rumbling from beyond the neighborhood.* OFFSTAGE *& at the end of the stage, there is a gathering of white cloth. The* HOLY GHOST PEOPLE ENTER *dressed in white flowing cloth. They are holding each other's hands; they are humming. They walk toward the brick apartment building, toward the lawn. The* SPEAKERS *crowd in the window of the apartment building, looking out, watching the* HOLY GHOST PEOPLE.

> HOLY GHOST PEOPLE *[walking across]* we do not feel cold.

> SPEAKERS so they say.

> HOLY GHOST PEOPLE *[stopping on the lawn]* this is fodder. a history of the gaze. or muted rhetoric. we do not feel cold.

SPEAKERS the holy ghost people claim they have let go, heaved us into the pith of cities.

HOLY GHOST PEOPLE god has let go. we have let you. we have heaved you into the pith of cities.

SPEAKERS though we were never in, nor heaved.

HOLY GHOST PEOPLE you are out. everything billows. we moved through star clusters for you. the breadcrumbs of photographs of stars—we will find our way back, but there will be nothing left, till something new forms between the dark matter. we will go on. there are other humans & we will find them when the ones we are meant to save are saved. there is darkness. dark matter cured the air. the orbit sack. *[the HOLY GHOST PEOPLE form a circle, clap hands, look up into the window]* everything billows. this banter will not be what identifies us.

SPEAKERS we are backlit in this conversation.

HOLY GHOST PEOPLE god protects us, projected us out.

## SCENE II

*SPOTLIGHT — The mall parking lot.*

*The HOLY GHOST PEOPLE have gathered around a small cluster of cars. They hum. They suddenly stop & clasp hands. The SPEAKERS roll their windows down, lean out.*

> SPEAKERS *[from their car windows, letting the cars run]* reframe. there are beautiful bodies under that white cloth. a whole flock of defectors leave their cubicle-light. reframe.

> HOLY GHOST PEOPLE you have fallen. you just cannot see the height of the fall. but it is galaxies tall. *[they begin to sing, melodic humming]*

> SPEAKERS oh jesus, they're singing.

> HOLY GHOST PEOPLE *[singing]* whenever possible conjure sylvia.

> SPEAKERS sylvia?

> HOLY GHOST PEOPLE sylvia is not here yet.

*A seagull squawks.*

> SPEAKERS *[laughing]* sylvia is that you?

> HOLY GHOST PEOPLE tactics. ethics. the why of it.

*There is humming coming from* OFFSTAGE.

*From the* DARKNESS.

## SCENE III

*SPOTLIGHT* — *The church.*

*The HOLY GHOST PEOPLE* ENTER *the light & stand in the garden. The SPEAKERS come to the door & stand. A woman in a blue dress appears in the center of the HOLY GHOST PEOPLE.*

SPEAKERS in the coax of skeleton trees a preacher is dying, repenting to the holy ghost people. the holy ghost people conjure sylvia. her dress is blue. the holy ghost people dance around the preacher. inside the trees. her dress is blue. why is it not white?

HOLY GHOST PEOPLE what you see as blue is just another shade of what you call white where we come from. sylvia wears the purest of whites.

SPEAKERS this is not church ritual. tracterians, ink-hands & bloat. they are at it. the holy ghost people have recruited. the weakness of faith revs. rules of brimstone & star-light & galaxy-flex. the lost in fog-light. smoke machines & smoke theatrics, but there is no smoke, no stage, just our lawns & courtyards & roads & & & & & &&&

HOLY GHOST PEOPLE broken parts must die, broken parts.

SPEAKERS but you are so right about them. they are not truthful & you look like your mother in the garage shadow.

HOLY GHOST PEOPLE you are all full of broken parts, but you hide it by always talking. sylvia wants to help you, because god wants to help you.

SPEAKERS this sylvia has been unconjured, vanished. who was that earlier? is that who you called sylvia?

*The HOLY GHOST PEOPLE begin to hum.*

SPEAKERS holy ghost people, what are those sounds? they are not words—

HOLY GHOST PEOPLE these are our words. we will translate:

SPEAKERS translate.

HOLY GHOST PEOPLE our lies are more truthful than yours. our lies end with your salvation.

## SCENE IV

*SPOTLIGHT — The playground.*

*Children* ENTER *the light & run around the playground. Their parents follow. On the other side, a clot of* HOLY GHOST PEOPLE ENTER.

> SPEAKERS they speak of time travel, of star clusters, of gods molding dark matter, of fossilized planet-marrow & dinosaur skins. they speak of this sylvia, again.

> HOLY GHOST PEOPLE of this, god touched. jesus is only a name. your name is only a name. they are the same. are you a part of god? god is not in parts. there is no holy spirit. no father, no son, no holy ghost. just god.

> SPEAKERS we realize that holy ghost people is a bad name for them. but we can't shuck it away. it clings. everyone still uses it. the holy ghost people are not ghosts. they have real hair. god loves them most, so they say. so they say. so god says. so they say. god lets them bend in the time-flux space travel, the galaxy flickers dust. they carry the dust in their hair, it makes them look red-headed. at night it looks like neon.

*SPOTLIGHT — The church.*

*The* HOLY GHOST PEOPLE ENTER *the light & walk toward the church.*

HOLY GHOST PEOPLE god will come for you in the ether-light of dreams, your throat will be slit in your living room, in your lawn, in the road, in your workplace, in your bed. when there is a dead owl without its feet in your back lawn, you have been judged & god is coming, or he is sending us to finish. you will know in the morning & god will come in the night & the owl will rise & you will be dead flesh. you'll ask for sylvia then.

# SCENE V

*SPOTLIGHT — The dive bar.*

*The SPEAKERS ENTER. There are only a few people inside, drinking.*

> SPEAKERS we didn't see them coming, but all of a sudden they were standing in our lawns, in our lobbies, in our hallways, in our traffic, in our courtyards, in our malls, in our restaurants, in our drive-throughs & they were wearing white cloth & they were speaking & speaking & speaking. did you see them conjure sylvia? she just appeared. who is she? what is she?

*The HOLY GHOST PEOPLE ENTER the bar; they are humming. They walk toward the SPEAKERS, softly touching the other patrons.*

> SPEAKERS check posture, you white throats. they call themselves that—or we call them that—

> HOLY GHOST PEOPLE *[stopping just in front of the SPEAKERS]* you may know the method, the truth, that nothing, what tense is this, in making?

> SPEAKERS & credit is due—those are ferns. the horseflies, dead in the barbeque, planters, ashtrays, carcasses on the porch.

> HOLY GHOST PEOPLE how is the test-imony different? if we give it back to history,

archive the truncated grammar & let your polaroid-gloom deaden time, then you will truly know boredom—33 million—33 million—

*A BARFLY picks up a camera. Begins filming.*

SPEAKERS turn that camera off.

HOLY GHOST PEOPLE turn that camera off.

## SCENE VI

*SPOTLIGHT* — *The apartment building.*

*The HOLY GHOST PEOPLE walk onto the lawn. The SPEAKERS stand in the doorway.*

SPEAKERS we build things we love to make this machine work. we're trying to make fire. radically, we know each other's languages—i knew something was happening. smug, gotta get to that clover. i'm not trying to holla, someone says. so, hinge into it. boom. yes, boom. if that's what sends me into stone, that's what sends me into stone. begin in the impact.

HOLY GHOST PEOPLE increase your threshold for pain. you can't shake it for jesus. no resurrection required.

SPEAKERS edmonds, the skipper, is boarded up, but we still smell the fried fish, the clam chowder & saltines.

HOLY GHOST PEOPLE get over yourselves, girls.

SPEAKERS what type of jig are we cutting?

HOLY GHOST PEOPLE essential tremors aside, you will unmake this river. you will unmake this humidity.

**SCENE VII**

*SPOTLIGHT — The dive.*

*A few SPEAKERS ENTER the kind of crowded room & sit at the bar. A BARFLY drinks.*

SPEAKERS *[to each other, at the bar]* one of them stops sermonizing, looks right at me, says—

*SPOTLIGHT — The apartment & lawn with the HOLY GHOST PEOPLE & the SPEAKERS in dialogue.*

HOLY GHOST PEOPLE we were born in a piano. the keys. the echo. our grandfather was a hummingbird.

SPEAKERS *[at the apartment]* the crosswalk, littered with wings & feathers & ivory flecks. you talk like a grad student, the way you dismantle language, instruct, the way you turn back toward the salt hills. the car, of course, is full of waits—& i'm not gonna lie. the snohomish river curves under us, feral, we can see a son gutting trout on the rocks. who put invention into existence?

HOLY GHOST PEOPLE a maze of disaster, distilled into an event—you say, collapse has a process, & point back to the road. you say, change can't unravel back into stasis. there's nothing you can do. that mail slot is blocked—

SPEAKERS transit into the trail—the detour, the hedge, the channel spike—you are so drunk when i pick you up & you want to see the floating bridge, the construction—you say, there's supposed to be an abandoned piano, abandoned train cars, filled with gravel & chunks of coal. you're asleep when we get to the bridge. i watch the construction lights from the hood, waiting for you to wake & demand a cigarette.

HOLY GHOST PEOPLE this feels like a mistake.

SPEAKERS smooth or striated, or not—if all language is appropriated, then you are oceanic. naming is an important part of this whole thing, but i cannot think of one for you. you want to talk about the striation of fact.

HOLY GHOST PEOPLE look, this is not double-work, an assignment, a photograph—tin-type—we've never seen photos. catalogue, catalogues. welter-sick, look at your shoes. sylvia would not approve.

SPEAKERS [at the bar, to each other] i said, no, we should watch the white throats, they're up to something. she said, they are harmless. i said, come.

HOLY GHOST PEOPLE *[at the apartment]*
evidence, evidence.

SPEAKERS *[at the bar, to each other]* we respond.
ok. evidence, evidence.

## SCENE VIII

*SPOTLIGHT — The mall parking lot.*

*The HOLY GHOST PEOPLE* ENTER *& walk up to a car, surround it. There are people inside. The SPEAKERS* ENTER *& stand behind them.*

SPEAKERS holy ghost people, i can see you making faces. holy ghost people, i can't see you move. holy ghost people say,

HOLY GHOST PEOPLE *[to the people in the car]* what have you gained from all those bible verses you memorized? god is not in those pages. god is unimpressed with its fiction & your memorization of fiction. it's like memorizing novels. it's like reciting lines from archaic novels. there is always a yellowing before sentences— *[turning to the SPEAKERS. The car doors open, three young women get out, hurry away from the scene.* OFFSTAGE, *we can hear them speaking, quietly, indecipherably. The HOLY GHOST PEOPLE address the SPEAKERS]* can you feel the desert in our syntax?

SPEAKERS i feel winter in those sounds. but it is winter when they come & they are dressed for desert life. is this it? or do i really hear winter spewing from their mouths?

HOLY GHOST PEOPLE sylvia has been absent since we first conjured her. she came & went. your lack of belief pushes her back out

into the dark matter. you can claim the dust,
the arroyos, claim the wasted sky of home—

SPEAKERS we drink from the same water.

HOLY GHOST PEOPLE we drink from the
same water.

SPEAKERS we drink from the same water.

HOLY GHOST PEOPLE we drink from the
same water.

SPEAKERS we drink from the same water.

HOLY GHOST PEOPLE we drink from the
same water.

SPEAKERS we drink from the same water.

HOLY GHOST PEOPLE we drink from the
same water.

SPEAKERS we drink from the same water.

HOLY GHOST PEOPLE we drink from the
same water.

SPEAKERS we drink from the same water.

HOLY GHOST PEOPLE we drink from the same water.

SPEAKERS we drink from the same water.

HOLY GHOST PEOPLE we drink from the same water.

SPEAKERS we drink from the same water.

HOLY GHOST PEOPLE we drink from the same water.

SPEAKERS we drink from the same water.

HOLY GHOST PEOPLE we drink from the same water.

SPEAKERS we drink from the same water.

HOLY GHOST PEOPLE we drink from the same water.

SPEAKERS we drink from the same water.

HOLY GHOST PEOPLE we drink from the same water.

SPEAKERS we drink from the same water.

HOLY GHOST PEOPLE we drink from the same water.

SPEAKERS we drink from the same water.

HOLY GHOST PEOPLE we drink from the same water.

SPEAKERS we drink from the same water.

HOLY GHOST PEOPLE we drink from the same water.

SPEAKERS we drink from the same water.

HOLY GHOST PEOPLE we drink from the same water.

SPEAKERS we drink from the same water.

HOLY GHOST PEOPLE we drink from the same water.

SPEAKERS we drink from the same water.

HOLY GHOST PEOPLE we drink from the same water.

SPEAKERS we drink from the same water.

HOLY GHOST PEOPLE we drink from the same water.

SPEAKERS we drink from the same water.

*Two POLICEMEN ENTER.*

POLICEMEN what's going on here?

SPEAKERS nothing, really. just these people spitting stories, lies probably.

POLICEMEN we got reports of some weird people being weird.

HOLY GHOST PEOPLE would you flush it out the airlock? god's justice implodes in the stardust. mutterings of the planetary formation. ice belts & oh our god had a mission. our god guides this mission. our hulls were breached when we entered the atmosphere. who punched a hole in the ice moon? we put it in a lunar orbit, fracturing the distance between the supernova & the milky way. & people want microgravity machines in the asteroid mines, but there are not asteroid mines because there is never anything to mine from asteroids & no microgravity machines because those are gateways to god's wrath. our lights puncture the dark sides of planets where people say god forgets, but god does not forget, not our god, god always remembers & god knows what's brewing in those sides.

POLICEMEN *[stepping closer]* move along, you…

SPEAKERS yeah, move along, white throats.

POLICEMEN white throats?

SPEAKERS sometimes we call them that.

POLICEMEN move along, white throats.

*The HOLY GHOST PEOPLE disperse. The SPEAKERS stand by the POLICEMEN.*

POLICEMEN *[to the SPEAKERS]* you too.

**SCENE IX**

*SPOTLIGHT — The farmers' market, full of people shopping, wandering.*

*The HOLY GHOST PEOPLE* ENTER. *The SPEAKERS* ENTER *from the* DARKNESS. *They gather at the front, facing each other.*

SPEAKERS the holy ghost people say,

HOLY GHOST PEOPLE all you need to make a star is tongue-baths & god's will.

SPEAKERS scientists immediately disagree. announce, all you need to make a star is hydrogen, gravity, & time.

HOLY GHOST PEOPLE time is not an ingredient. & all you need to kill a star is truth-serum from the mouth of a sparrow & god's undoing of the past.

SPEAKERS scientists immediately disagree. announce, all you need to kill a star is iron. that is rain in the photo.

HOLY GHOST PEOPLE the universe was milky, before, before, before. so, if iron is poison to a star then a star is a man. a star is not a man, therefore, a star cannot be killed by iron.

SPEAKERS scientists, iron can kill a star in seconds. we've seen it happen.

HOLY GHOST PEOPLE you have not seen stars die. we have. you are lies built on a foundation of intentions. sick, sick, sick, blasphemy. time will gut the lies from you. you'll see.

SPEAKERS the holy ghost people say,

HOLY GHOST PEOPLE stars can only be killed by the blood of god. that is how he undoes the past. blood. clotted blood. though he is made of blood, so there is no cut to be made, he just drips into a star. that kind of undoing. so if you want god to rise keep contradicting him. he will drop his blood into your star before it should explode. wait, he will show you if you don't unspeak these lies.

**REST.**

Reframe.

SCENE X

TIME - WHENEVER

*SPOTLIGHT* — *The dive.*

*A handful of SPEAKERS at the bar, drinking.*

> SPEAKERS *[to each other]* can you hear it in the meat of their songs? fire escape watchers. the sunlight washed in the cheap digital camera. the holy ghost people look like angels with halos around their entire bodies, the cluster of them. halos & halos' halos. but it's just the camera being shitty. cinderblock attention. give me a name unlike jesus, please. *[a few HOLY GHOST PEOPLE ENTER. The SPEAKERS do not notice]* the missive burns in the lawn. they are removing them from mailboxes, lighting them up. the oceanographer turns into a holy ghost person, denounces her work. she looks beautiful in their white cloth. gaze. we have seen her naked through windows. we have memorized it. gaze. reframe. gaze. her body is. she blends into the mass of cloth. we cannot see her body, only the whole of the gathering. speak on, they speak on, her voice becomes a part.

*The HOLY GHOST PEOPLE approach the SPEAKERS.*

> HOLY GHOST PEOPLE *[stopping behind the SPEAKERS]* when we speak it's explosive.

*The SPEAKERS stop drinking, turn around.*

**SCENE XI**

*SPOTLIGHT* – *The church.*

*The HOLY GHOST PEOPLE & the SPEAKERS in dialogue on the church lawn. The conversation goes.*

SPEAKERS holy ghost people!

HOLY GHOST PEOPLE the world is already a suicide. we didn't come to catalogue your faults, but we will if you need us to. judgment is not for us, it has been ordained by god. we will catalogue only if you need us to, the judgment, though, will not be ours.

SPEAKERS you say, everything billows.

HOLY GHOST PEOPLE yes, everything billows.

SPEAKERS the holy ghost people fell in love with matches. not for fire. for the smell. they can make fire with their hands. so they say. they did not come for navel gazing. gaze, again. they speak of white dwarf stars so dense they will sink through the earth. they say,

HOLY GHOST PEOPLE that is how hell was made.

SPEAKERS hell, apparently, is not metaphysical—

HOLY GHOST PEOPLE who is not to be-lieve? the place of forests bordered by desert stretches. a place of forests is known. vista rock blocks the wind. you will see it if you repent. blunt honesty? god doesn't not love you, but there are depths to his pity. listen: the wind tells.

SPEAKERS i suppose.

HOLY GHOST PEOPLE oh god, this is what you think it means to learn to love? love is only for god. there is no spirit, no son. as we have said. he wants to make lives together, but you won't let him. god wants to show you love, but he has grown tired & that has turned to pity. so much pity stacked up. he can't love you anymore. so we will show you love in his stead. maybe there's a chance. but at least our love is floating in the space between our hearts & your cold-blood.

**SCENE XII**

*SPOTLIGHT — The beach.*

*The HOLY GHOST PEOPLE* ENTER *from the* DARKNESS. *They wade into the water. The SPEAKERS* ENTER *from the* DARKNESS. *They toe the shoreline. We hear the sound of waves, seagulls squawking.*

SPEAKERS what color are those eyes?

HOLY GHOST PEOPLE color? they are the color of sylvia. you would not comprehend it.

*The sounds continue.*

**SCENE XIII**

*SPOTLIGHT* — *The dive.*

*Full, with two SPEAKERS sitting at the bar drinking beer. The SPEAKERS continue to drink. A BARFLY drinks.*

SPEAKERS pipe smoke & pipe smoke & pipe smoke. mahogany. they wait for us. they want us to live in log cabins on forest moons or in adobes on desert planets pocked with watering holes. there will be a middle of a forest or an oasis or—there will be homes, they promised, tucked in the mountain passes of other planets. holy ghost people. holy ghost people. holy ghost people. truths, they want us to believe.

**SCENE XIV**

*In* DARKNESS, *we hear the HOLY GHOST PEOPLE speak.*

HOLY GHOST PEOPLE we fled an exploding star. god sent it, but he told us first. he told us the star was exploding & that we had a task. we fled the orbit of our galaxy & behind us, we watched the star unload.

*SPOTLIGHT* — *The playground, full of* HOLY GHOST PEOPLE *&*
*SPEAKERS*.

HOLY GHOST PEOPLE desert planet, we
said, desert.

SPEAKERS but it is winter here.

HOLY GHOST PEOPLE we still need water—

SPEAKERS we drink from the same water.

HOLY GHOST PEOPLE we drink from the
same water.

SPEAKERS we drink from the same water.

HOLY GHOST PEOPLE we drink from the
same water.

SPEAKERS we drink from the same water.

HOLY GHOST PEOPLE we drink from the
same water.

SPEAKERS we drink from the same water.

HOLY GHOST PEOPLE we drink from the
same water.

SPEAKERS we drink from the same water.

HOLY GHOST PEOPLE we drink from the same water.

SPEAKERS we drink from the same water.

HOLY GHOST PEOPLE we drink from the same water.

SPEAKERS we drink from the same water.

HOLY GHOST PEOPLE we drink from the same water.

SPEAKERS we drink from the same water.

HOLY GHOST PEOPLE we drink from the same water.

SPEAKERS we drink from the same water.

HOLY GHOST PEOPLE we drink from the same water.

SPEAKERS we drink from the same water.

HOLY GHOST PEOPLE we drink from the same water.

SPEAKERS we drink from the same water.

HOLY GHOST PEOPLE we drink from the same water.

SPEAKERS we drink from the same water.

HOLY GHOST PEOPLE we drink from the same water.

SPEAKERS we drink from the same water.

HOLY GHOST PEOPLE we drink from the same water.

SPEAKERS we drink from the same water.

## SCENE XVI

*SPOTLIGHT* — *The dive, again.*

*Many more SPEAKERS gathered, standing away from the bar.*

> SPEAKERS there are temples. there are tow-
> ers. there are shafts of light & stained glass.
> there are foxes & wolf cubs. there are lilies
> & rose stems & pollen & old wasp nests.
> there are straps from moving trucks & hand
> trucks. there are metals & alloys & flawed glass
> bubbles, wrinkles, cracks from time & pressure.
> the holy ghost people say there are starships
> colliding & there are wormholes. there is no
> sylvia.

*In DARKNESS, the HOLY GHOST PEOPLE speak.*

> HOLY GHOST PEOPLE there are worm-holes. we jumped through them. there were starships colliding with orbiting planets & dwarf planets & asteroids & moons & we survived because god wanted us to say this to you. to tell our story & show you that your bibles are full of lies. whenever possible we will conjure sylvia, but it is not possible if you won't listen. listen to us, we know space & what it's like to stretch across a galaxy & through an asteroid belt of frozen water. if you listen, we will conjure sylvia. we will conjure that language-maker to offer coordinates. sylvia will offer the next path. we will find her in the field when she is ready. though we have seen her, we have, in our time, denied her. but you, you must be willing to listen before you are willing to deny her. to deny without consideration is only a folly on the precipice of extinction.

## SCENE XVIII

*SPOTLIGHT — The church.*

*A clot of HOLY GHOST PEOPLE standing outside the church.
The SPEAKERS exit the church, approaching them.*

SPEAKERS don't talk of cosmos. i want to
see the atom-flex, the way planets collide when
a galaxy forms, orbit slack & ice planets, moon-
dust & asteroid-clash. but you want to talk
more about your god than your journey. tell us
about the space you cut through. we do not
care about what your god claims. deep breaths.
knuckle-white. flexed biceps & calves.

HOLY GHOST PEOPLE jesus walked, but
you drive & ride trains, buses. that seems sloth-
ful. & even though jesus is not god, is just a
man, & the real god's never heard of him. that
seems like you can't even cling to your own
religion. it's all, oh but he's a god. rather than,
how can i do what he does? human capacity
for faith is limitless, but you all, you give up at
the get-up. if you have faith, hold that. hold it.
faith is a sphere of glass if you want it to be.
maybe it looks like a white dwarf star radiates
inside of it. that's what faith is to us. & when
we get faith, god hands it to us, so we can hold
it. we do not let it go, we carry it. we are not re-
minded of it, because it is a thing we can hold.
we do what we do because we hold faith. it is
tangible. your god does not believe in tangible
things. science believes in tangible things, but

science only proves that men believe they are smarter than god, & till they realize they are not, god will not go without punishing them in death. you think you're so smart. science is a broken faith, but you all cling to it. it's either that or your god & we all know what that is.

SPEAKERS give us the good stuff. the black tongue & stomach deep. give us the army jacket & stairwell run. the dresser of good booze. the holy ghost people parade. the holy ghost people preach. sermon-flare. the snake handlers have been bitten, give into the holy ghost people. the tv's waving lights ruptured in four.

HOLY GHOST PEOPLE you can't junk your way out of this. you can't. this is god's way of setting the record straight. what are you looking for? this planet aches toward a tilt. you sinners are unholy & chatter-rogue. rumor-mill, gossip-lit. your bodies/our bodies are not the same. your bodies breed recklessness in evening temperatures. our bodies, vessels. god knows the insides. knows our organs & blood pulse. impurity is nothing but a dent in our movement. god cleans us when he checks. he knows the shape of our limbs of our extremities of our sexual organs. he knows, oh he knows the ridges, the creases, the way they move & rise & bulge in the heat, in pressure, in lust. sins forgiven.

sins upheaved. sins unpacked. sins stacked. confessional-booth sins. pew-sin. bible-sin. salt-sin. the garden-sin. marriage-sin. father/mother-sin. children-sin. sunday morning-sin. saturday-sin. weekday-sin. science-sin. idol-sin. god-sin. religion-sin. sin-machines—hear them? sin-machines clot the highway, the parking structures. sin-machines in the atmosphere, in the heavens, in the orbit. sin-machines killing. sin-machines. we will kill the sin-machines. they will not bleed. go easy. go lightly. go forth.

SPEAKERS goddamn you reckless preachers. you holy ghost people, ending lives.

HOLY GHOST PEOPLE the star cluster unlocks from orbit. we are waiting for the collision. atmosphere hooks. that is god letting go of you. repent, sin-machines. that is god letting go one finger at a time. that is not sylvia. when sylvia gets conjured your time to repent is over. so listen, this is the time to unlearn what you've carved into yourselves & relearn what truth we're bringing.

SPEAKERS sylvia means nothing in this conversation. we know nothing of her or what she brings. & the mass of window-dirt & the mass of our sexual bodies hide your lies from us. the mass we embrace. through the window—

HOLY GHOST PEOPLE lust-machines. sin-
machines.

SPEAKERS the holy ghost people have spoken.
the holy ghost people are known.

## SCENE XIX

*SPOTLIGHT — The mall parking lot, a few cars parked.*

*The HOLY GHOST PEOPLE move through the parking lot, speaking.*

> HOLY GHOST PEOPLE we left our sins in the open airlock. they became rings orbiting gas planets. the moons spiraling volcanoes. our sins, our sins. will you let your sins go? will you put them in the airlock? we will open the hatch & they will become pieces in orbit or pieces between dark matter & moons. sylvia is silent. muted somewhere out in the nebulas. in the hull-light, god comes to us. she can't be conjured.

**SCENE XX**

*SPOTLIGHT — In a clearing, surrounded by skeleton trees, there is a hunk of metal with a door.*

*The HOLY GHOST PEOPLE move in & out of it, others sit on the ground outside, eating & praying & talking. A few SPEAKERS stand at the edge of the light, behind the trees, watching.*

SPEAKERS there is a clearing where the holy ghost people come from. we find it because we followed them out of the city & into the forest. at night it glows at the center. flickers. this is not a spaceship, but in a past life it could've been. how long have they been here? did we not notice till now? who are they really? the mass of metal is a hump in the center of a clearing. holy ghost people go in, come out, go in, come out. they have gathered around it. made homes, tents, wood, teepees, campfires. a colony buzzing. but the buzz is so quiet. at the center, there again, the ember-red light in the hull. is that a hull? the holy ghost people are singing now. one of them holds a sphere in her hand, kneels, looks into the night. we watch. they mumble, but they keep calling for sylvia. they speak the name like you might a god's. we dredge assumption back into our brains. tell by the weight of it. there are more of them. some return from the city to sleep, others leave. they are singing. they are dancing. they are preaching. they sing *sylvia come to us, sylvia we believe it is time to move.* others are going. others are coming. others. others. others. others. others.

**SCENE XXI**

*SPOTLIGHT – The apartment building.*

*The HOLY GHOST PEOPLE* ENTER *from* DARKNESS *& stand in front of the apartment. The SPEAKERS stand in the doorway.*

SPEAKERS the helix curves & they have stories about it. about what happens when a star bursts & how fast you must travel to escape it. the burst of helium. the final heat. & boom. & the holy ghost people claim they saw 17 stars die before they made it here. they say god wanted them to know, to see that eventually the sun will unlock & life will scatter or get swallowed in the burst. they are serious against bibles. in stores they have bought them all, in churches they go missing. some say they have burned down the bible factories, the warehouses of bibles. emptied hotel drawers. some say they saw a pile in the field just before the forest wall. say, you should've seen the way those bibles burned. we challenge the holy ghost people. say, if god sent you, what does he look like? if god sent you, why are you frail? & why have you failed? the laugher. oh how they laugh. the holy ghost people, all smirk-looking.

HOLY GHOST PEOPLE god needs us to fail. the majority of you will die in the burst of this star, or burst when god squeezes the liquid out of this rock, but we have not seen god. no one has seen god. god is not seen. god unleashed. god hides & uses his extremities to punish. he does not have a face. your bibles lie. if we said we have seen god we would be liars & nothing we say would be true, but we have not seen god, because god cannot be seen, therefore we are truth-tellers. we are not liars. we don't even know how to. it is not in us. unlike you, bred to lie, we can smell dishonesty in your blood. we must purify. so, we have not failed. the ones who are capable of purification will follow us, the rest of you will do as you must & become corpses & gravestones. god heaved us into the spotted black of space just as we are charged to heave the pure of you out with us, into that uncertain flux of the universe, rubber-banding out & out & out. god, oh god he wants us to heave all of you out, but he knows, he knows we will fail & wants us to. therefore it is not failure, as god already knows it. his population will be a controlled one. we are the original humans. sylvia knows this. soon she will show you. yes, we are the original humans.

**REST.**

Reframe.

**SCENE XXII**

*SPOTLIGHTS RISE, revealing the neighborhood. No one is on stage. A handful of SPEAKERS ENTER. They are dragging a body through the neighborhood. It is a HOLY GHOST PERSON. They drag it across stage.*

*OFFSTAGE, we hear the SPEAKERS.*

    SPEAKERS what do we do with this body?

**SCENE XXIII**

*SPOTLIGHT — The dive, nearly empty.*

*Two SPEAKERS are in quiet conversation. They drink.*

> SPEAKERS we hid bodies in the cake. & me, i'm still clinging to the throb of it. swallowing that kind of logic? there are white cloths flapping. those do not sound like hymns, but they are singing—what is that frequency? we want to know sylvia.

**SCENE XXIV**

*SPOTLIGHT* – *The farmers' market, winding down, very few people.*

*The HOLY GHOST PEOPLE & the SPEAKERS ENTER from the DARKNESS then stand close, in dialogue.*

> SPEAKERS holy ghost people what do you call yourselves? the holy ghost people do you call yourselves such? the people want to follow. people want to know of the second coming.
>
> HOLY GHOST PEOPLE this is the first coming. there is no second coming, because there never was the first. god sent us. know that. rip it away. the future choked back into the present. time is a bent circle. anyone can travel the circle, god willing.
>
> SPEAKERS they are here to make us feel bad. they are here to show us our sins.
>
> HOLY GHOST PEOPLE we are not concerned with bible textures, a simple god is what there is. intended to unravel.
>
> SPEAKERS logic will unlatch at the people. ethos as technical jargon. pathos as heart-strung. logos as watchdogging the data-curl. where is logic?
>
> HOLY GHOST PEOPLE it is logic. listen.
>
> SPEAKERS in the middle & another kid wants

proof, but that was not a spaceship, but that was a hull & there were holy ghost people crawling from inside. where are they coming from? who are they?

HOLY GHOST PEOPLE who are you?

SPEAKERS if god sent them, we must repent. but god did not send them, so we must not repent.

HOLY GHOST PEOPLE if there is a crack in the hull, then the dwarf planet will sink through the earth. the ability to travel galaxies is not technologically impossible in this time, therefore god must be.

SPEAKERS they did not come from space, they are frauds. the church says this. the church claims they want their gold. & the holy ghost people wear white cloth. they speak loudly— but they are not aggressive. the voices cushion into us. lacerations. fingerprint smudges. blood-son. there are dead holy ghost people in the church hallways. their blood is not like our blood. they have no blood. their blood are nebulas. they are gathering. they speak.

HOLY GHOST PEOPLE the blood will draw us into the end. we will travel into time with the repenters. we will rapture back into the galaxy shift, out of orbit, where the next star cluster hides the next planet. god is done with you. god will let go. he lifts his hands & yet you kill us. blood. blood. but our blood is not like your blood. we can feel the blood spilling. you spilled it.

*SPOTLIGHT — The church.*

*The HOLY GHOST PEOPLE mill around the church garden. The SPEAKERS listen, at first.*

HOLY GHOST PEOPLE this moment ruled us—now it is the serpent's turn. such shade & kings & comet-flare & yes, all that dark matter. into, into, into. into the black fathoms. increase your threshold for pain. this is more fodder & god has let go & everything billows & you still want sylvia, though you pretend not to know, but we will not/cannot conjure sylvia. & she is not here because everything billows & god is not in parts & never was & 33 million, 33 million, 33 million. but you will not uncode this, you will listen & let it fall, but there is something unloading into this planet, centuries before that big star explodes. wake up & listen to our warnings. you are running out of chances, running out of warnings. god is not the most patient, no matter what your script-ures give you. they are just lies written by men. everything billows, everything.

SPEAKERS *[moving closer]* you white throats, you're good at letting fear into every scene. but you are white throats, you are the ghost of a religion most of us have laughed away. your god is no god, your god is a story punched together with astronomy & pop-astrophysics & we do not believe you, because there is nothing to believe.

your story is laughable. you are humans & you are laughable. no one, no god has sent you. so, we will laugh you away.

## SCENE XXVI

*SPOTLIGHT — The beach.*

*The sound of waves crashing. The HOLY GHOST PEOPLE stand ankle-deep in the water. The SPEAKERS toe the shoreline, waiting for them to finish.*

*The HOLY GHOST PEOPLE preach & the SPEAKERS wait for their turn to respond. There is no one else on the beach. A dog runs through. There is a whale out in the water.*

*Seagulls squawk.*

HOLY GHOST PEOPLE put away those gadgets. answer this: what is the orchestration of planetary formation & why is this planet lacking in collision damage? god is the answer, but your scientists say it was made this way without the touch of god. your god did not make this universe. see, our god made it. our god let it happen, he holds it & one day he will let go. this planet would be a flat sheath of rock if god wanted that. but it is round, it moves & orbits & our god bursted life into every seam of this planet that was once nothingness, held on & gave us causation. only now he needs us to see this.

SPEAKERS telescopes see no god.

HOLY GHOST PEOPLE seeing is never believing & telescopes only see dot sin in the massive fathoms of black. look at your heaps of metal & glass. your use of alloys comes from other voices & others' ideas. & yet you let the alloys speak for you—

SPEAKERS you speak as if what you say is fact. we have learned to recognize cults.

HOLY GHOST PEOPLE a cult is nothing more than a gathering of opposers. a cult is what the status quo calls the others. you fear cults because they can unhinge what you've set as truths. cults are good. they make you learn how to doubt the best things. but it is your god that is a product of cults. we are just people sent by god.

SPEAKERS many of us believe there is no god.

HOLY GHOST PEOPLE now that is laughable. & blasphemy is ignorant. but you've seen enough & still you deny.

SPEAKERS blasphemy only exists for believers.

HOLY GHOST PEOPLE belief is irrelevant, whether you believe or not doesn't make something not there. the sun will explode & space is cold & even if you deny it, these are truths.

SPEAKERS but those things can be proven.

HOLY GHOST PEOPLE we can prove our god. but you would deny it still.

SPEAKERS give us proof & we will listen & look & consider.

HOLY GHOST PEOPLE your kind of proof is guess-work & ungodliness, our proof you will fail to understand as proof—you have failed this whole time.

**SCENE XXVII**

*The HOLY GHOST PEOPLE* ENTER *from the* DARKNESS *&*
EXIT *into* DARKNESS.

*The SPEAKERS, in* DARKNESS.

> SPEAKERS while they're singing someone
> shouts, there is no god! & the holy ghost
> people rise. they are limbs & white cloth & for
> once, fury. they are not peaceful.

## SCENE XXIX

*SPOTLIGHT – The beach. Barely any waves. Quiet. A seagull squawks.*

*SPOTLIGHT – The dive. Jukebox music plays. The SPEAKERS lean close to each other. A BARFLY drinks.*

*The HOLY GHOST PEOPLE & SPEAKERS in the separate locations, in dialogue.*

> HOLY GHOST PEOPLE god does not support peace when blasphemy slithers around.
>
> SPEAKERS the holy ghost people find the strangest of things blasphemous: bibles, crucifixions, dalmatians, great danes, orange cats, nikes, paleontologists, hair braids, cocaine, mirrors, horses, snakes, egg shakers, egg beaters, diet soda (except pepsi), pickup trucks, red pens, paper cuts, dogs smaller than 10 lbs, people who don't believe in time travel, gold, silver, red light bulbs, energy saving light bulbs, hybrid suvs, parkas, flip phones, thongs (both kinds), smoked salmon, alloy bats, the sci-fi channel, alt-country, nu-metal, bark in playgrounds, dead pigs...
>
> HOLY GHOST PEOPLE the claustrophobia of time travel. it takes something out of you & puts god in there, but we are strong. we love to feel pieces of him kicking at our rib cage. we have a mission. *[they pause, look around, like they're waiting for something]* buckshot nebula. there are 47 planets orbiting a superstar & they pass within

3000 miles of each other & it's hell to get through it—planetary orbit-shake & the way a planet unhinges flight plans—but getting around it would take years. see, it was a test from god. he wanted to see if we could make it through it—no it is not like the disciples & jesus. this had nothing to do with the bible or sons or doves—this is about god testing us. but of course unlike you, so flawed, we were made to trust & we move through the orbit. on the other side we could see the milky swath of this galaxy, the dot of your star burning in the center. this would be our first stop. sylvia will not listen to you, nor will she listen to us.

SPEAKERS who is sylvia? you people keep talking about sylvia & she is not here. can you conjure her again? show us! bring her back!

HOLY GHOST PEOPLE we will not con-jure sylvia. we cannot. you have made it un-so. sylvia is not a person, not a being, but an idea. sylvia is the doubt we have. sylvia allows our faith to multiply, build in us. sylvia is that sliver of thought questioning the holy ghost people, sylvia is the thing that turns us back to the real god. not your god or any god you worship.

SPEAKERS someone says, they conjured sylvia. but i cannot feel sylvia. the holy ghost people are coming. they come with sylvia. my friends are watching them. we are trapped in our homes.

HOLY GHOST PEOPLE trappings are man-made. sylvia does not perform in such ways—you have known her words for ages. you all just don't know it.

SPEAKERS [at the bar, to each other] the black gum of night. we've memorized their schedules. the steps. the holy ghost people are asleep & we move past them, into the hull darkness, but we turn back.

HOLY GHOST PEOPLE he will not turn you into salt, but he will press you into the core. molten. you will sink. there will be no flood because god doesn't want any more water on this orb. god knows you know how to swim & water wouldn't be final enough. your bodies were made to float. the trinity? blasphemy.

SPEAKERS [to each other, at the bar] somebody kills a holy ghost person & when they talk about it they speak of his weightless body & how there was no blood when he was struck & how only oak spikes could hold him down & how you must choke them—striking does nothing, stabbing does nothing. you must choke the breath out of them. there is no blood. only air. according to new literature, the holy ghost people eat grass & co2 & melted tar from construction sites & gravel. they do not bleed because there is only air in them. god would never make a being as such—they must be devilish. they must embody evil. they must be liars. we watch them from warehouses. take notes. there is something about them that we don't understand & the hunk of metal in the forest clearing is not enough. we got close, but inside there is no light. from outside it looks as though there is. now we follow them. we watch them & at the end of the week we get together to share what we've noticed. even the way they walk is something. gliding steps. & with their white cloth it looks as though they are floating. but they're not floating. they can't be. there are humans who have turned to holy ghosts. but they are alive & they never floated before, but now it looks as though they float. it must be the cloth. it has to be. someone says, we should kill a convert. see what happens. this is not decided to be a good idea, but on their own someone kills one & like the other ghosts there is no blood. there is only air & a choking death.

*A very long silence.*

*DARKNESS.*

**SCENE XXX**

*STAGE LIGHTS FLICKER, STROBE, revealing all locations.*

*There is no one.*

*Moments pass, THE STROBE CONTINUES.*

*HOLY GHOST PEOPLE ENTER. They move around all of the scenes, walking in a single file line, all over the stage, weaving.*

*SPEAKERS ENTER. They move around all of the scenes, walking in a single file line, all over the stage weaving, in different routes than the HOLY GHOST PEOPLE.*

*THE STROBE INTENSIFIES.*

*The SPEAKERS & HOLY GHOST PEOPLE move more swiftly, breaking up, moving around the stage, swarming & swarming & swarming. There is a blur of bodies & white cloth.*

*No one speaks.*

*They just swarm.*

*A very long silence.*

*STROBE QUITS.*

*LIGHTS FALL.*

*DARKNESS.*

**SCENE XXXI**

SPOTLIGHT *reveals the clearing & all the* HOLY GHOST PEOPLE *gathered outside the hunk of metal. Inside something glows. Outside, the* HOLY GHOST PEOPLE *are humming.*

*The* SPEAKERS *gather at the edges of the* SPOTLIGHT, *watching the* HOLY GHOST PEOPLE.

*As they watch, the* HOLY GHOST PEOPLE *begin to move into the hunk of metal disappearing from view.*

*The* SPEAKERS *watch till there is no one else left.*

*A few of the* SPEAKERS *follow the* HOLY GHOST PEOPLE *into the hunk of metal.*

*Others do not.*

*Moments pass.*

DARKNESS.

*The* HOLY GHOST PEOPLE *hum. It crescendos to the point of distortion.*

*The scraping of metal.*

*The crunch of tree & stone.*

*Sounds fade.*

*Moments pass.*

*A long, pregnant silence.*

**REST.**

**CURTAIN FALLS.**

**JOSHUA YOUNG** is the author of *when the wolves quit* (gold wake press), *to the chapel of light* (mud luscious press), and, with chas hoppe, *the diegesis* (gold wake press). he is the associate director of poetry & nonfiction at columbia college chicago. he lives in the wicker park neighborhood with his wife, their son, and their dog.

**HI-FIVES** to the faculty at Columbia College Chicago (especially David Trinidad, for saying "Whenever possible conjure Sylvia [Plath]" which set off this manuscript and Ken Daley, for giving me a job as well as fodder for this); my cohorts (especially Daniel Scott Parker, who first told me this was a play); Ryan Spooner, for his support of this project and for designing this cover—you beast; Elliot, who gives me a reason to do anything; Em, for supporting me from the beginning and being an undying inspiration in my life—you make me want to be a better man; Tyler, for taking this monster and helping me carve out the play/poetry; my family and friends; CAConrad; Nick Courtright; Madeline ffitch; Carmen Giménez Smith; Connie Voisine; Tony Trigilio; Jennie Fauls; Nicole Wilson; Jared Wahlgren; Matthew Shenoda; Sam Weller; my father, Mike Young; and you, for buying this play.